Leaning into Life

Lois Shank Hertzler

Nashville - ABINGDON PRESS - New York

LEANING INTO LIFE

Copyright © 1974 by Abingdon Press

Library of Congress Cataloging in Publication Data

Hertzler, Lois Shank, 1927-
    Leaning into life.

Poems.
I. Title.

PS3558.E79514   811'.5'4   73-21534

ISBN 0-687-21297-9

Manufactured by the Parthenon Press at
Nashville, Tennessee, United States of America

For
Elam
husband and friend

Foreword

It is not uncommon to find a person who can use words in beautiful ways. It is not uncommon to find someone who can pray with great power, expressing the heart's deep hunger for God in moving and authentic ways. It is extremely uncommon, however, to find both of these gifts in the same person, yet that is what is so obvious and impressive about these meditations.

They are written with the artist's love of beauty and can be enjoyed for their literary quality alone. As you read each one you find yourself caught up in the rhythmic movement of the words and carried along by the flow of ideas and images. If "a thing of beauty is a joy forever," then these meditations will bring great joy to many persons for they are beautiful in this way.

After we have finished reading them, however, there is something that remains with us, something more than the echo of well-chosen words. We come away feeling that we have been skillfully guided into a deeper relationship with God. Here are authentic expressions of the heart's deepest desires for communion with the God who offers us wholeness of life beyond our fondest dreams if we will respond to his loving presence in our lives. But we need to know how to respond, how to express our feelings, what to say. What a joy to find ourselves saying things to God in these meditations which we have been wanting to say for a long time, but didn't know how.

In our church we have been using them in our

private prayer times and in our prayer-study-action groups. I am overjoyed to know that so many others will now be helped and inspired by these words from one whose spiritual roots are deep and whose literary fruit is so delightful. Read on and enter into the joy of your Lord!

Edward W. Bauman

Acknowledgement

I wish to acknowledge my gratitude to family and friends whose suggestions proved most valuable to me in putting together this book, particularly Kay, Carol, and Elam. Most especially, I wish to thank Dr. Edward W. Bauman through whose encouragement this book came into being.

Lois Shank Hertzler

Leaning into Life

Am I my brother's keeper?

A figure lay huddled
on the warm grillwork
clothes tattered and smelling
lifeless hair, matted and blowing
grimy skin of unknown color.
The empty eyes moved
and looked at me
as I hurried by.
I wondered
what blew out the spark?
what happened to the dreams?
how was hope lost?
Isn't there someone, God,
who will pause long enough
to dust off the dreams
to make alive the vacant stare
to awaken hope?
Don't look at me, God,
you know how busy I am
with your work
just like others of your children.
It really is too bad, God,
one of your children hurts
and there is no one
to care enough.

**Treat others as you would like
them to treat you.**

Help me see
the lovely in the unlovely
for there is much
that is unlovely in me.
Help me see
the beauty in the dull and the drab
for there is much
that is dull and drab about me.
Help me see
the excitement in the common and the ordinary
for there is much
that is common and ordinary about me.
Help me see
the perfection in the imperfect
for there is much
that lacks perfection in me.
Help me see
the good in others
for there is much
that is good in me.

**Be ready for action with belts fastened
and lamps alight.**

A mind that is open
I find hard to keep
for too often there enters
criticism of others
that corrodes my thinking;
prejudice toward others
that blurs my vision;
apathy of spirit
that limits my horizons;
and so my mind becomes cluttered
with much that is useless
unimportant
destructive.
Let my criticisms turn
to honest praise
my prejudices change
to compassion
my apathy waken
to action
so that my mind becomes a channel
for that which is positive
loving
and kind.

**Keep your tongue from evil and your
lips from speaking deceit.**

The need to examine my concept of honesty
has been dogging my waking moments
with increasing persistence.
I wonder,
God,
if there are times
when you would have me be less than honest.
I wonder
if honesty can be sharply defined
or if it swings somewhere between the extremes.
I wonder
if my concept of honesty reflects your mind
or
if it is warped by my own prejudiced opinions.
Sometimes
to be totally honest
seems cruel and brutal.
I find it takes courage
to be honest
and I'm not always courageous.
Clear away
the mental debris
that clutters up this area of my thinking.
Be the guiding force
in each moment of truth
so that my "Christianity"
does not create a credibility gap
for those with whom I mingle.

Let your yea be yea and your nay, nay, lest ye fall into condemnation.

I fudged a bit
on the truth one day
not nearly enough to say
that I had actually lied.
Then I found to my amazement
it was really quite easy
next time around
to stretch a word
into two or three
to rearrange a line
or so
to shave a wee bit off
here and there
until one day
I was horrified to find
that I who told the tale
no longer knew
just where the real truth lay.
I didn't think it mattered, God,
they were such tiny points,
how important truth
as truth can be
until I made a liar
out of me.

**Pride ends in destruction,
humility ends in honor.**

We clasp our hands
we sing
we shout
how great we are
we, the liberated
we, whose bonds are broken
we, who have let go traditions
we, who are the contemporaries
we, who are free.
Stop us, God,
before we become
more entrenched than the entrenched
before we become
more traditional than the traditional
before we become
more bound than the bound.
Help us, God,
to mingle
the old with the new
for a unifying blend
of all your people.

For where your treasure is there will your heart be also.

We hide in our building
we call it a church
we say we're God's people
whose claim is to be
different in spirit.
We give of our money
sparingly, that's sure,
but enough so our conscience
gives us some peace.
We give of our time
the frayed part, that is
when our bodies are fatigued
and our minds rather numb.
Forgive us the leftovers.
Our priorities, it seems,
have slipped out of line.
We forgot that the church
is more than a building.
We forgot that your people's
giving must be
of self, time, and money
all three.
We forgot that you want us
your ambassadors to be.
So make of us a people
of whom it can be said
truly, they are
God's people
in thought, word, and action.

**Cleanse first that which is within the cup
and platter that the outside of them
may be clean also.**

Inaccurate labeling
is a charge made true
when in pressing
for selfish interests
I assign them to you.
When fearing to delve
into issues controversial
I cop out with the statement
I relinquish all to you.
When refusing responsibility
for behavior not the best
I turn around my thinking
and place the blame on you.
In actions that are cowardly
and words that are untrue
I find "agape" handy
in faking my way through.
Help me change my labels
to make them accurate
that I may in honesty live
with each and every one
of all my fellow men.

If thou, Lord, shouldest keep account of sins who, O Lord, could hold up his head?

My country
is she right or wrong?
If all I do
is stand and noisily condemn her
or stand and shout, "she's right"
I only add another voice
to an overwhelming din.
But if I would change her
the change must start with me.
I may disagree with her stated priorities
but do I honor my own?
I may disavow her values
but have I laid claim to my own?
I may abhor her prejudices
but do I still nurse old hatreds of my own?
My country
whether right or wrong
makes her no less my country
but if I would improve her
the improvement must begin
in me
for I cannot expect her
from my living to gain
what has not yet
become true of me.

**Thou wilt keep him in perfect peace
whose mind is stayed on thee!**

Attune my mind to the thought
that your cause is weakened
when I allow feelings of envy and jealousy
to overpower me,
be they envy of another's possessions
or envy of another's job,
envy of another's relationships,
or envy of another's abilities.
Examine with me
my motives and attitudes.
Clear my thinking to understand
that when my eye wanders and fastens
with unreasonable desire
on what another has or is
that I am blocking my own source of supply
and hindering my own ability to receive.
In asking only for those things
which in your plan for me are mine to have,
I am freed from
anxieties,
fears,
jealousies,
and angers
that are generated by too much looking.
Let not my greed
become a stumbling block
in the unfolding of your plan for me.
In the pain of working through new discoveries
I find there is growth
toward my becoming more your person.
And for this I am grateful.

For as he thinketh in his heart so is he.

As a seed is planted
in fertile soil
with the sun for warmth
and raindrops for drink
so a thought is born
deep in my mind.
It bursts forth
full blown, strong,
flowering into action
protected by an inner watch
guarding my mind.
I understand, God,
how in my thoughts
lies buried the person
I later become.
Grant me wisdom,
all-knowing One,
to sort well the seeds
produced in my mind
to prepare well the soil
used
to nurture the person
you created me to be.

Forgive us our trespasses as we forgive those who trespass against us.

Sometimes, God,
I find it hard,
very hard
to forgive.
Give me
the spiritual maturity
to comprehend
that when I am persistent
in remembering and condemning
that I am permitting myself
to be warped and enslaved
by my own thought patterns.
Give me courage
to let go of past memories
knowing that what is past *is* past
and that the future
need not be tarnished
by the remembrance of deeds from the past.
Deepen my understanding
to know that
you have given me freedom,
freedom to move away from these emotions
that have the potential
to consume my vitality,
blind my vision,
and destroy my relationship with you!
Thank you,
God,
for helping me find my way through
the painful realities
that are so much a part of living.

When anyone is united to Christ, there is a new world, the old order has gone, and a new order has already begun.

I would be free, God,
free of beliefs
holding me imprisoned,
free of hatreds
influencing my health,
free of jealousies
threatening my loves,
free of insecurities
annulling my identity,
free of fears
undermining my peace,
free of prejudices
dulling my vision,
free of desires
enslaving my appetites.
I would be free, God,
free
just to be me
the "real me"
who has been given birth
by my union with thee.

I will hear what God the Lord will speak.

I am so used to myself as I am, God,
that I need insights
into how and in what areas I need to grow.
My mind races off in a dozen directions
to avoid quieting down,
to avoid a direct encounter with you.
Forgive me
for charging ahead,
thinking I know the answers,
without consultation with you.
Forgive me
for throwing up blocks
that prevent the flow of your power and love
through me.
In this listening silence
may I be able to perceive
with understanding and conviction
your guidance
in the hour-by-hour transactions of daily living.
The silence becomes alive
as the vacillation of wanting and not wanting
settles into a period of expectant calm.
I begin to understand with a new clarity
that God speaks—
through a friend,
that God speaks—
through an experience,
and that God speaks—
in the silence,
and that it is I
who am not listening.

Wait for the Lord, be strong, take courage.

A part of life
hard to see
is that it's just not for me
to do God's part.
I don't manage very well
my own responsibility.
Still I run ahead and try
manipulating
coercing
impatiently fretting
when answers I have sought
are not in my view
forthcoming.
As time moves along
I learn to let go
preconceived notions
of my life's arrangements.
I learn for me
my need is to be
open and receptive
freeing me to see
God's good judgment
always waiting for me.

Where is your faith?

I failed today, God,
failed to reach another
for whom the meaning had gone from life
though my caring for her was real
her ability to respond and feel was lost
for the storm had been too intense
rolling over her
battering and bruising her
leaving her with senses numbed
her will to recover dulled.
Casual acquaintances ignore her
friends have forsaken her
relatives have rejected her
so she built her walls high
closing off all avenues
through which love might touch her.
Where will she turn now, God,
she rejects me
she rejects you
she rejects herself.
Dark night surrounds her
tormented and alone she wavers
between living and dying
love seems to have lost.
You know, God,
and I know
that love is never lost,
but how do we let her know
when her desire to know
lies buried in the ruins
of her shattered life?

Lo, I am with you always.

How sad to be lonely
in a crowd
or by oneself.
How sad to be adrift
alone without a guide
where the tomorrows hold no challenge
where yesterday was only bleakness
where today is no more than a stretch of time
between yesterday and tomorrow.
Bring us together, God,
those locked in loneliness
or lost within themselves
or isolated by desire;
those friendly and caring
wishing to give and share
that our world might be a friendly place
where griefs and joys are shared
where everyone is part of life
and one in spirit
then loneliness need plague no one.

In him we live, move, and have our being.

Direct my powers of receptivity
inward
that I may draw
my feelings of worth from you,
my source.
Hold close to me
the knowledge
that you are the activator of my life.
Enlarge my understanding
to know
that my ultimate happiness need not become
confused or splintered
if comfortable friendships
and familiar surroundings
do not continue to fulfill my expectations.
Increase my ability
to realize
that while my inner security may be enriched by,
it should not be dependent on,
the "goings on" in my environment.
How good it is to know that
you are the answer to my search for identity!
How good it is to be alive,
really alive,
and to know
I have a source,
a source that is always
receptive,
giving,
and loving!
Thank you.

Then shall your light break forth like the dawn.

I need aloneness
daily with thee
to know myself
and who I am
to find an identity
to iron out wrinkled thinking
to establish inner calm
to search for daily guidance
to know that you are you
that you care about me
enough
to stay near by
through each uncharted day
of nitty-gritty living.
Change my base of operation
from reaction out of fear
to a response
growing out of
an awareness of your presence
so that
where I am
you are.

In the world you will have trouble. But
courage! The victory is mine;
I have conquered the world.

The night was to have been
a family celebration
until she told him
she had found another
for whom she cared
although their life together
had spanned two decades
she never really cared
he was just a convenience
that fit her style
and so she had used him
to fill her need
of money, social status, and desire.
Her physical death
he could have survived
but to see her in the arms of another
while his own lay bare
crumpled his world
around his feet
self-confidence gone
ego dismantled
a broken man.
In time he would pick up the pieces
and rise above the pain
but for now
he could only
hope
to endure.

**If we live, we live for the Lord;
and if we die, we die for the Lord.**

It isn't whether I smile
when the day goes right
but whether I can still smile
when the going seems all wrong;
It isn't whether I'm friendly
to all my friends
but whether I'm still friendly
when I feel snubbed and ignored;
It isn't what I am
in periods of calm
but how I react
in periods of stress;
It isn't whether I love
when I'm loved in return
but whether I still love
when none is returned;
It isn't whether I forgive
when forgiveness is sought
but whether I forgive
when trespassed against
that speaks to the truth
of my being for you
a channel that is open,
seeking, and true.

A good name is more to be desired than great riches, esteem is better than silver or gold.

Her cane
her slow gait
her silvered hair
age-mellowed skin
speak of her many days
and many years
of gathering wisdom
while learning to smile
when needing to cry
of learning patience
when lacking same
of learning to love
when there was none
of learning to trust
an all-wise God
who carried her through
thick days
and thin.
I admire her courage
her well-rounded living
her many years
her life that to me
is an inspiration
God-given.

If anyone wishes to be a follower of mine he must leave self behind.

Patience is a virtue
I'd like to call my own
not something merely desired
but part of my living.
To be patient
a minute or two
I can be disciplined to do
but when time drags on
and the need remains
I begin to fret and complain
about the drain on me.
Patience that is enduring
standing by to the end
is a mark of spiritual maturing
a goal for every man.
I will be content to grow
step by little step
until I reach a point
where it is safe for me
to take a larger one
for so it seems to me
that only a giant
can safely take a giant step
and I am not a giant
. . . yet.

Rejoice with those who rejoice,
weep with those who weep.

How good it is
to be part of a "caring" community.
How good it is
to feel the rhythm of life
that flows in the warmth of human relationships.
How good it is
to feel the revitalization and fullness of life
that comes as with others,
openness is sought.
How good it is
to experience with others
a deep sense of your nearness.
In this inspired atmosphere
it becomes
a privilege rather than an obligation,
a sacred responsibility rather than a duty,
to stand beside another
who finds the going rough,
or to stand beside another
who finds joy spread in his way.
Increase my understanding
of the oneness with others
that comes
as my own relationship with you deepens.
Permeate all my human contacts
with your living presence
and with your love.
Thank you, God,
for being my friend.

Jesus wept!

I wonder about death, God,
it waits for us all.
Even though one's wish is not
to respond to its call.
She was beautiful, glowing
in looks and in action.
I cherished her friendship
our fondness was mutual
but death came and took her.
Then I wondered about death
she wanted to stay here
with all who were dear
to share life with them
young, vibrant, and full
but death came and took her.
Then I wondered about death
they said it was cancer
that shortened her stay
one spring morning, early
before dawn of day
death came and took her.
I wonder about death, God.

It is good to give thanks unto the Lord.

As a warming ray of sun
reaches through the chill
of an early morning
so the awakening awareness of your nearness
reaches through the doubts and indecisions
clouding my mind.
Thank you, God,
for the little things in a day full of living—
the white velvet of a fresh magnolia blossom—
the caress of a playful breeze
during the heat of the day—
the scolding cry of a noisy bluejay—
white fluffy clouds drifting in a sky of blue—
the vivid color of a cardinal flashing by—
contagious laughter drifting in through an open
        window—
the twinkle of recognition in the eyes of a friend.
Gratitude lifts my heart
and I am aware that
there is good in everything
even though at times
I am unable to sort it out.
Surging up from deep within
a quiet serenity spreads
through my entire being.
For the beauty of your presence,
I thank you.

Give, and it will be given to you.

Depression colors my day
in differing tones of gray
obscuring my desire for you.
Cut through thoughts that are gloomy
with confidence renewed
in your presence.
Help me see
that giving myself
to the simple events
that make up my day
causes happiness to rise
penetrating the murk
giving light to the eye
and a spring to the step.
Show me, then,
how laughter is a feeling
rather than an empty sound
as you take control
of the ups
and the downs.

Rest in the Lord and wait patiently for him.

To be a "now" person
is my real desire.
So stay with me, God,
as I spend time removed
from the hue
and the cry
of noise-filled days
and too short hours.
Draw me apart,
Restorer of all,
to repair
frayed edges
and ruptured calm
with a strong sense of Presence
deep in my center.
Reveal yourself, God,
in this day's intermingling
of myself with others
whose needs I am often
too insensitive
to discern
in my nearsighted view
of the movement of time.
Slow me down
that I might be
more actively
in tune with thee.

**Gray hair is a crown of glory
and is won by a virtuous life.**

In this land gone wild
on a cult known as "Youth"
our balance has been lost
between growing old gracefully
and not growing old
for it seems a disgrace
to admit
to years over thirty.
We spend many dollars
backing off the years
removing the wrinkles
coloring the gray
being unduly absorbed
with the physical body
betraying our memories.
We miss much that is beautiful
charming
alive
in the veneration of age
with its beauty of spirit
its wisdom
gained through experience
its loves
that have been tried, fulfilled.
Give us grace
to admit to our years
in joy
mingled with pride
for each new one
that we add.

Rejoice in the Lord always, and again I say rejoice!

With increasing awareness
I find I have been
long on petition
and short in gratitude
during periods of communion with you.
My heart sings
in the beauty of your presence,
yet I seldom verbalize the joy I feel.
Peaceful satisfaction calms me
as the realization that you are,
becomes clear to me,
yet I seldom take time to tell you so.
The knowledge
that you care that I am,
never ceases to amaze me,
yet I seldom take time to express my deep
    appreciation.
I have taken for granted
that you, being you,
know how I feel.
I have failed to understand
that verbalizing my feelings about our relationship
will deepen and season it,
causing me to be
more open
and more trusting.

Forgive, God,
my lack of sensitivity,
my preoccupation with other things,
and my failure to be consciously grateful.
Develop in me
the joyful habit
of being daily
thankful in all things.

God opposes the proud but gives grace to the humble.

I find it very difficult
to take a close look
at the person I am.
I do not want to admit
to myself
as I am.
I plant myself firmly in your way
and then wonder why
I'm not more aware of you in my total life.
I want my pet projects and theories
regardless
and connive to manipulate you out of the picture
and then wonder why
you sometimes seem remote.
I become impatient
and charge ahead
delaying your active participation
and wonder why
you are so slow in responding.
I am swept low
with disappointment
when something of importance to me fails
and I wonder why
you have let me down.
I wonder why—
and with painful clarity
the reply shatters the silence—
I have said
"my way,
not yours."

Watch lest I follow any path that grieves thee; guide me in the ancient way.

I desire to be free
but do I give freedom
or do I cling
like the proverbial vine
to someone
and call it love;
or do I enslave
with my demands
that others fit
my cherished molds
and call it love;
or do I scoff
at the thinking of another
because it is out of line
with mine
and call it love;
or do I reject persons
because their life-styles
differ in degree
from that which pleases me
and call it love?
Tell me, then,
is it in the giving of freedom
that I who seek it
find it
and will I know it as love?

Search me, O God, try me, and know my thoughts.

Walk with me, God,
into the shadowy area of my thoughts.
I am afraid of the person I find there.
When your light penetrates this self-enclosed area
I find I'm not the kind of person I thought I was
nor am I the person my friends think me to be.
With increasing clarity
I begin to understand why
you cannot work more effectively through me.
Help me
to relinquish feelings of anger, jealousy, and hate.
Help me
to understand how to deal with them,
how to acknowledge their existence without
permitting them to usurp control.
There is pain—
pain that I shy away from
in facing this needed change in my own person.
As I accept the knowledge
that this too is me
and that it is because of your love for me
that you desire to help me move forward,
then the way is open for your power to move in
and strengthen my desire to overcome.
I suddenly realize
I do not carry the weight of my ungodlike traits
alone
for you are beside me
and gratitude floods my soul
bringing with it
the abiding peace of your presence.

**The Lord knoweth the thoughts of man,
that they are vanity.**

There is this enemy, God,
who most adamant can be
while stealing a place
deep in my mind
when I carelessly let slide
the daily discipline
of quietly centering in.
Although he is very subtle
his off-shoots are not—
they corrode and block
and would finally subvert
my association with you.
That is why I ask you, God,
to examine well with me
my motives
and my attitudes
before
those with a negative bent
gain permanent control of me.
You see, God, I find
as I plod along
this enemy of mine
perched up there
on his self-proclaimed throne
turns out to be
none other than
the "I" in me.

**And great multitudes followed him and
he healed them all.**

Places of healing
greet one
with antiseptic smells
whisper-shrouded voices
and the quiet tread of rubber-soled shoes.
Are you here
as anxiety mounts
and blossoms into naked fear?
Are you here
when relief breaks
over a sweat-stained face
as good news is brought?
Are you here
in this place
where death walks hand in hand
with life?
I remember
you told us
your contact with us
is us.
So you ARE here
unless
we have closed the door.

If you have ears to hear, then hear.

Healing that I seek
whether of mind, soul, or body
does not always come
in the degree I desire
because I lack the know-how
to be open to it
in unadulterated form.
Answers that I seek
whether personal, job, or group
do not always come
in the manner that I crave
because I lack the insight
to be open to any other
than the one
I have preconceived.
Guidance that I seek
whether for myself or another
does not always come
with sure direction
because I close my mind
to the openness I need
for thinking that is generated
from sources other than my own.
My problem seems to be
that while I am willing to seek
I am not willing to find
help in any form
other than that which pleases me.

**God moves in a mysterious way
his wonders to perform.**

There has come to me a quiet beauty
in a growing relationship of cooperation
with you, God.
I have found it hard to put aside
whimpers of self-interest.
I have found that
I indulge in intellectual dishonesty
to avoid
having to give up some of my pet theories.
I am happy, God,
happy that we are friends,
not because of my human weaknesses
but in spite of them.
So I am grateful
for the insights you have given me,
I am grateful
that you forgive my wanderings,
I am grateful
that you are patient with my arrogances,
I am grateful
for the sense of direction you have given me.
I do not know how to express adequately
my inmost feelings
in the delight of your presence.

It has been good
searching for and finding
an upward surge of consciousness
of searching for and finding
my relationship with you deepened
of searching for and finding
the movement of your Spirit
already at work.
Thank you, God,
for everything.

No one lights a lamp and puts it in a cellar.

I looked at the faces
I passed on the street
some open, some honest,
some reflecting deceit,
some smiling, some laughing,
some sorrowfully sad,
some strained, full of tension,
some wholly cast down.
I stopped short in my musings
a question flashed in my mind.
What were those passing me
on the street
reading in my face?
Was it radiant, full of joy,
or was it covered
by a mask of indifference
because of my fear
to let happiness flow through
to the faces I meet
while passing on the street.

The earth is the Lord's and the fullness thereof, the world and they that dwell therein.

Thank you, God,
for your love's vitality
that surrounds me
as I roam through your world.
Thank you
for soft raindrops
for warming rays of sun
for gentle breezes
all making joyful preparation
for the return of life
one feels pulsating
through slumbering nature.
Thank you
for your promise
of a pageantry of color
hidden in the swelling bud
and the fragile sprig of green.
Thank you
for the end
of winter's long silence
brought by
a bird's lilting song
and a cricket's muted chirp.
Thank you, God,
for everything.

Never flag in zeal, be aglow with the Spirit, serve the Lord.

I am grateful
for the intellectual knowledge
that you are present in sluggish periods
as well as in periods of high awareness.
You see, God,
I've been immersed
in the spiritual doldrums—
I simply have not felt receptive.
I've just drifted along
with formless thoughts
and empty actions.
Help me remember
that a meaningful relationship with you
requires discipline
even when I don't feel like being disciplined.
Dissolve my fatigue
and let me be open to your strength
that I may be uplifted.
Gather in my thoughts
and let me be open to your wisdom
that I may have understanding.
Guide my actions
and let me be open to your control
that I may be directed.
Move in my spirit
and let me be open to your love
that I may be healed.

Then Jesus beholding him loved him.

I noticed the light
and wondered why
so I stopped by the door.
It startled me to find
a young man asleep
in a stiff office chair,
lank body all folded
chin resting in hand;
the hour was so early
his sleep was so deep.
Why was he there, God,
had he no place to go?
His face in repose
all bare of its mask
revealed a sadness
so deep
that I stood still in awe.
I knew he would soon stir
and I wanted to be gone
for I felt ill at ease
to have viewed private pain.
I reached out to you, God,
with a prayer from my heart
for the stranger asleep
in the stiff office chair
before tiptoeing
quietly away.

Commit your work to the Lord, and your plans will be established.

Flying kites
carefree children
butterflies
dandelions
buzzing bees
where will they go
as man with his machines
tears at the earth
leveling, uprooting, destroying?
Show us, God,
how to
compromise with nature
while meeting our needs
before we become
a land of mortar-laced bricks
and acres of concrete
with no room left
for
flying kites
carefree children
butterflies
dandelions
buzzing bees.

God saw everything he had made, and behold, it was very good.

I saw a flower opening today, God,
the first of its kind this season
golden center
reflecting the glow
of the evening sun
white petals fluttering
as a breath of air sped by.
I was saddened, God,
for as I looked
I saw tarnish marring the gold
and flecks of soot on the white
evidence of man
with his exhaust fumes
and belching smoke stacks
dwarfing and maiming
nature's children.
Help us, Creator,
to overcome this blight
we have foisted
on one another
before it turns
and
smothers us.

Be ye transformed by the renewing of your minds.

As the tide of eternity flows on,
may I not drift with the current
but rather give myself
to your great pattern of beauty
in my todays and tomorrows.
Heighten my personal awareness of your guidance
coming through a host of conflicting desires
in my inner life.
Alter the shape of my mind,
expand and saturate it
with the integrity that comes from
communion with you.
Lift me out of the mire of self-pity,
cleanse and renew my spirit.
Forgive me for taking so much for granted,
for forgetting to be grateful.
Forgive me for sinking my anchor of security
in the material world so often.
In deep gratitude
I thank you that you are,
that you care that I am,
that you understand when I hurt,
and that you continue to care
even when I become convinced of my own clever-
     ness.

Reverence awes me as the beauty of your love
flows into me with new meanings.
I realize anew
that the way to Eternal Truth is challenged only
by my inability to accept guidance.
My heart swells with thankfulness
as the barriers I throw up dissolve
as you become master of my moods
and your creative power surges in.

The Lord is my shepherd; I shall not want.
He maketh me to lie down in green pastures:
he leadeth me beside the still waters.
He restoreth my soul.

May I draw on the thought that
deep within me you have created an island of calm
to which I can withdraw
and relax in the awareness that you are.
Free me
from the rigidity of impatience.
Let not the pressure of deadlines
stiffen and make brittle my thinking.
Give me
the strength to let go
of my human conception of time
and my compulsive desire to hurry.
Restore my capacity to rise above my inadequacies,
to renew my commitment,
and to react creatively to reverses.
Deepen my level of understanding
and increase my openness
to receive new insights into myself
and my behavior.
Give me the courage to look quietly,
intelligently,
and realistically
at those insights.
Show me the difference between
your guidance and
my own deep-seated desires
that I try to label "Divine."
May I know the deep contentment
that comes from renewed commitment
as
I move forward under your direction.

**Trust in the Lord with all thine heart
and lean not on thine own understanding.**

There are times, God,
when the tyrant, anxiety,
moves in with rapid stride
threatening to override
my ability to cope
with this puzzle
called LIFE.
I would look up
so that I might find
your steadying hand
reaching out
pulling the commonplace
into perspective again.
Increase my faith
that trust might grow
granting me serenity
in periods of stress
and renewal of strength
in periods of calm
for so often I find
things going wrong
and I wonder why
until I discover
my trouble to be
caused by
my trusting in
ME.

He who is not with me is against me, and he who does not gather with me scatters.

Faith in you, God,
for me has come hard.
Too often I have placed
my wavering trust
in some one of us.
Eventually I have learned
that each one of us
at one time or another
has feet made of clay;
we say one thing
but bank on another;
we mean well it seems
but we look to a wrong source,
for faith placed in one another
may come totally unglued
in times of deep need.
The harder we try
the more trauma we encounter
until turning to thee,
our ultimate source,
we find strength supplied
in abundance
for every need.

Abide in me and I in you.

Thank you
for ability to respond positively
to life's changing scenes
preventing body energies
from being unduly sapped.
Thank you
for awareness of your movement
overcoming my shallowness of spirit
with a new spiritual depth.
Thank you
for awakening my response
to your love
enlivening my slowness of heart
with an inner guidance.
Thank you
for wisdom overpowering
my stubbornness of mind
increasing my ability to be
a channel through which
you can touch others.
Forgive me, God,
the times I resist
wholeness of any kind
for I realize thereby
I sanction again
the crucifixion
of your son
Jesus, the Christ.

**He gives to all men life and breath
and everything.**

I don't know why, God,
I oft push aside
much better wisdom
on the spur of the moment
to justify my pride.
Too often I find
concern for others
not my first choice
while commitment to you
stands wavering between
total and not sure.
Concerns and commitments
I studiously avoid
although at the same time
wanting to be
your total person.
How happy I am, God,
that friends we can be
not because of my wanderings
but because
you love me.

And the king will answer—I tell you this, anything you did for one of my brothers here, however humble, you did for me.

I almost spoke to her, God,
the young girl
so remote,
so alone in her grief.
I hesitated
afraid to intrude
so I walked on.
It still haunts me,
her face so expressive
her pain so recent
her valiant attempt at control
so frequently interrupted
by trembling lips
unbidden tears
shaking hands.
Was I wrong
to smother the impulse
to reach out
with a kind word
a touch of the hand?
I left her there
with only
a cigarette
and a cup of coffee
to ease her pain.
I'm sorry, God,
now—
that I moved on.